# Jesus

## The Real Story

This book was given
with love to

...... DANIEL STEWART ..

on

1.7ᵗʰ JUNE 2018 .......

by

EFFIE - SUNDAY SCHOOL TEACHER .

# Contents

# Note to Reader

This book is to help children discover more about Jesus. As you read these stories with them you are not only sharing vital time together, but you are sharing the Word of God, you are discovering Jesus. In this remarkable person we have both God and man – the creator who became the created. The Lord of life willingly died on the cross and rose again for his people whom he loved. As you read this book you are introducing your child not to a fictional character, not to someone who is distant and withdrawn but to one who was in every way like us – yet he was without sin. From the cradle to the grave and then the resurrection morning – these facts prove that God is love and that he is with us. Though our sin put the sinless one on the cross – his final prayer, "Father forgive them," is for us too.

Discover the real Jesus.
Focus on God's Word.
Go beyond the stable.
Discover the Truth.

# Jesus the Child

Mary was a poor young woman who lived in the village of Nazareth.

One day an angel came to tell Mary, "You are going to have a baby boy. You will call his name Jesus."

Mary was afraid at first, but the angel told her that the baby was the Son of God.

Joseph was engaged to Mary. When he heard that Mary was expecting a baby, he was worried too. God sent Joseph a message in a dream.

"Do not be afraid to marry Mary. The baby is God's Son. You will call his name Jesus, which means Saviour."

Joseph was happy to marry Mary then.

Mary and Joseph had to travel to Bethlehem to be counted in the country census. Bethlehem was so busy, they could find no room at the inn.

They spent the night in the stable and there baby Jesus was born. He was carefully wrapped up and a manger was used as his cot.

An angel of God appeared to some shepherds in the fields near Bethlehem. "I bring good news. Today a Saviour has been born in Bethlehem."

The shepherds hurried to Bethlehem and found Mary and Joseph and the baby lying in the manger. They praised God and passed on the good news to all they met.

When the baby was eight days old, he was given the name Jesus. Later he was taken to the temple in Jerusalem and presented to the Lord God.

A godly old man called Simeon held the baby Jesus in his arms. He realised that this baby was the promised Saviour. "I have seen God's salvation," he said.

An old lady called Anna then saw the baby Jesus.  She spent all her time praying.

She gave thanks to God when she met the special baby Jesus. She passed on the good news to all the people she met.

Wise men from the East came to the city of Jerusalem looking for the king of the Jews. King Herod was worried about this.

The wise men were guided by a star right to the house where Jesus was. They gave him beautiful gifts of gold, frankincense and myrrh.

They realised that he was the Son of God.

An angel warned Joseph in a dream. "King Herod wants to kill the young child."

Joseph, Mary and Jesus went to live in Egypt until the danger was past.

The family settled in the village of Nazareth
where Joseph was a carpenter. Jesus grew
up there with his brothers and sisters.

When Jesus was twelve years old he went with his parents to Jerusalem to celebrate the Passover Feast.

When it was time to go home a large party of friends and relations set off back to Nazareth.

After travelling for a day neither Mary nor Joseph could find Jesus.  In a panic they hurried back to Jerusalem.

After three days they found him. Jesus was in the temple sitting with the doctors and teachers, talking and asking questions. Everyone was amazed at his answers.

His mother began to scold him but Jesus said,
"Did you not know that I must do my Father's
business" He was meaning his Father God.

Jesus went back to Nazareth with Mary and
Joseph. He was a good, obedient, son. He
always pleased God his heavenly Father.

As he grew older he grew even wiser. Jesus said lots of wonderful things. His mother Mary thought about what he said.

# Jesus the Healer

A nobleman came to Jesus one day begging him to help his son. The nobleman's son was very ill. "Please come before my child dies," the man begged.

Jesus said, "Go back home. Your son will live."

The nobleman believed Jesus' words. When he reached home his boy was better. The fever had disappeared at exactly the time that Jesus had spoken to him.

Four men decided to take their sick friend to Jesus. They carried him on a mat to a house which was so crowded they could not get in.

They climbed up to the roof, made a hole in the ceiling and lowered the man on the mat down in front of Jesus.

"Your sins are forgiven," Jesus said. "Get up and walk." He was healed immediately.

A man with a withered hand met Jesus in the synagogue one Sabbath day. Jesus knew it was right to do good things on the Sabbath.

He said to the man, "Stretch out your hand."
The man found he could do that. His hand
was strong again.

An important soldier had a very dear servant who was very ill. He asked Jesus to come and save him.

"Just say the word and my servant will be healed."

Jesus was amazed at his faith. The servant was healed at that very time.

Jairus asked Jesus to come at once to heal his little girl. When Jesus reached his home, he said, "Do not be afraid, only believe."

He went to the room where the girl was lying. "Little girl," he said, "get up!"

Immediately she got up and walked about. "Get something for her to eat," Jesus ordered.

On the way to Jairus' house Jesus was delayed by the crowds. Someone came up close and touched the hem of his cloak. Immediately that lady was healed of her disease.

"Who touched me?" Jesus asked.
    The lady owned up fearfully. "Your faith has made you whole. Go in peace," Jesus answered her.

A woman from Greece came one day to Jesus. "Lord help me!" was her prayer. Her daughter was very troubled and needed Jesus' help.

The disciples tried to send her away but Jesus cured her daughter. When she got home the girl was lying peacefully on her bed.

A blind man was brought to Jesus. Jesus put saliva on his eyes and put his hands on him. "Do you see anything?"

"I see men that look like trees walking," he replied.

Jesus put his hands on his eyes again and he was completely healed. The blind man could now see clearly.

A deaf and dumb boy was very ill. He was so ill he would take fits. This would make him fall in the fire or into water.

When his father nervously approached Jesus, Jesus said, "All things are possible to him that believes."

The father cried out, "I believe; help my unbelief."
Jesus healed the little boy completely.

Ten men met Jesus.  They all had the skin disease leprosy.  "Jesus, have mercy on us," they begged.

Jesus healed them all. They had to go to
the priests to show them that they were all
better. Only one came back to Jesus to say
"Thank you."

Blind Bartimaeus sat by the roadside begging. One day he heard that Jesus was coming along the road. "Jesus have mercy on me," he shouted.

Jesus stopped and called him over. "What do you want?" he asked.

"I want to be able to see," Bartimaeus replied.

Jesus touched his eyes and he could see.

# Jesus the Miracle Worker

Jesus and his mother Mary were guests at a wedding in Cana in Galilee. Jesus' special friends, the disciples, were there too.

During the wedding feast Mary said to Jesus,
"The wine is finished."
   Mary then told the servants, "Do whatever
Jesus tells you."

There were six big stone water pots in the room. "Fill these up with water," said Jesus. "Now take a cupful to the man in charge of the feast."

The man thought it was the best wine he had ever tasted. Jesus had turned the water into wine.

One evening Jesus and his disciples were in a boat crossing the Sea of Galilee. Jesus fell asleep on a pillow in the back of the boat.

Suddenly a fierce wind blew up and the boat started to fill with water. The disciples were scared. They woke Jesus up. "Lord save us. We are going to drown."

Jesus stood up in the boat and spoke to the wind and waves. "Peace, be still!"

Immediately the wind died down. The sea
became calm. The disciples were amazed
at Jesus' power over the wind and sea.

One day Jesus and his disciples went to a quiet place for a rest but a huge crowd of people followed them.

Jesus was concerned for them. "Where will we get food for them to eat?"
Andrew answered, "There is a boy here with five little loaves and two small fish."

The big crowd of five thousand men plus women and children sat down on the grass. Jesus took the little picnic lunch and gave thanks to God.

He broke off pieces of food and the disciples handed them to the people. Everyone had enough to eat. There were even twelve baskets full of crumbs gathered up afterwards.

Another time a large crowd of four thousand men plus women and children had been with Jesus for three days listening to his teaching.

They needed food. All the disciples could find were seven small loaves and a few fish. Jesus again fed the whole crowd and seven baskets of leftovers were gathered.

Then there was the time that Jesus left the disciples to go and pray to God, his father. The little boat carrying the disciples across the lake was battered by the wind.

But then in the middle of the night the disciples noticed a figure walking towards them on the water. They were terrified.

"It is I," said Jesus. "Do not be afraid."
Peter wanted to walk on the water too.
"Let me come out to you," he said.
Peter climbed out and started to walk
to Jesus.

But when he saw the big waves he was afraid and started to sink. He shouted out to Jesus who caught him and they both went into the boat.

Then one day Peter needed money to pay his taxes. Jesus told him what to do. "Go to the sea and throw your fishing line in.

Take the first fish that you hook and look in its mouth. You will find there a piece of money – enough to pay for you and me." Peter did this and was able to pay all his taxes.

Jesus helped Peter lots of times. One day
when Peter was fishing Jesus told him,
"Put your boat out to sea and let down
your nets."

"We have caught nothing all night,"
replied Peter, "but I'll do as you say."

They caught so many fish that Peter had to call for help to pull in the net. The net was so heavy it broke with the weight.

# Jesus the Teacher

Jesus taught in lots of places. When he preached everyone was amazed at his knowledge.

He taught out on the hillsides where large crowds followed him to hear his wisdom. He even used a fisherman's boat as a platform to teach the people on the shore.

Jesus taught wonderful truths about God and heaven and how to live.

The disciples were arguing about who was the greatest in the kingdom of heaven.

Jesus called a little child over. "The one who is as humble as this little child is the greatest in the kingdom of heaven." He said.

When mothers took their children to Jesus, the disciples wanted to turn them away. "Allow the children to come to me," said Jesus, "for the kingdom of heaven belongs to people like them."

Then he took the children up in his arms and blessed them.

One dark night a leader called Nicodemus
came to ask Jesus some questions. Jesus told
Nicodemus many wonderful things.

"God loved the world so much that he gave his only Son so that anyone who believes in him shall not perish but have eternal life."

At the well in Samaria Jesus asked a woman for a drink. The woman was surprised. Jesus knew all about her.

"It is not where we worship God that is important," Jesus told her, "but how we worship. We need God's help to worship him as he wants."

Jesus tells us to pray to God who cares for us just like a father cares for his child.

If a child asks his father for a piece of bread,
he will not give him a stone instead. If he asks
for a fish he will not give him a snake.

Jesus taught us a special prayer we call
the Lord's Prayer.

"Our Father, in heaven
Hallowed be your name.
Your kingdom come.
Your will be done in earth
as it is in heaven.

Give us this day our daily bread.
And forgive us our sins as we forgive
those who sin against us.
Lead us not into temptation.
But deliver us from evil."

There is only one way to heaven. Jesus tells us, "I am the way, the truth and the life. No one can get to God the Father except by me."

"I am the door," Jesus said another time. "Those who come in through me will be saved."

"I am the bread of life," said Jesus. "No one coming to me will ever be hungry again, and the person who believes in me will never thirst."

Only Jesus can satisfy the needs and longings that we have in our souls.

"Which is the most important commandment?" Jesus was asked one day.

"You must love God with all your heart and soul and mind and strength." Jesus replied.

"The next one is that you must love other
people as much as yourself."

Peter asked Jesus, "How often should I forgive someone who sins against me? Perhaps seven times?"

"No, not just seven times," replied Jesus, "but seventy times seven."

Keep on forgiving those who do wrong to you. Treat other people the way you would like to be treated.

# Jesus the
# Story-teller

Jesus told lots of good stories.

    One day he told a story about a farmer who was sowing grain in his field. Some seed fell on a path and birds ate it.

Some fell on rocky soil and withered and died. Some seed was smothered and choked by the weeds. But some seed fell on good ground and produced a good crop.

Jesus explained the parable.

The seed is like the word of God. Some people do not understand and Satan snatches the word away. Others listen joyfully to God's message but when trouble comes they forget it.

Sometimes people completely ignore what God says – they care more about themselves. But some listen to God's word and understand it and their lives make God happy.

Once Jesus told an amazing story about a Jew who was on a journey from Jerusalem to Jericho.

All of a sudden he was attacked. Robbers took his clothes and money and left him badly injured by the roadside.

A Jewish priest came along but he passed
by on the other side of the road.  Another
came along.  He did not help either.

A Samaritan man then came along. He poured soothing medicine on the injured man's wounds and bandaged them. He put the injured man on his donkey and walked along to the nearest inn.

The next day he left money with the innkeeper to cover the costs. The Samaritan was the only one who showed love to the injured man.

Then Jesus told a story about a man who had one hundred sheep.

One sheep got lost so the man left the other ninety-nine sheep and went to search for the missing sheep.

When he found it he was so happy. Jesus told the people that there is joy in heaven when one lost sinner is found and trusts in Jesus.

"A woman had ten valuable silver coins," Jesus said. "One went missing so she lit a lamp and swept the whole house carefully. When she found it she called her friends to rejoice with her."

Jesus then told the people that there is joy like that in heaven when one sinner says sorry to God.

Jesus then told a story about a loving father who had two sons.

One day the younger one asked for his share of his father's wealth. He left home and wasted all the money.

When his money was done, a famine came
to that country. The young man was starving.

He got a job looking after pigs and was so hungry he felt like eating the pig's food.

One day he came to his senses. "I should go
home to my father. His servants are better off
than this." He set off for home.

His father saw him coming a long way off and ran to welcome him. "Bring out the best robe. Get him shoes and a ring."

A big party began. "My son was lost but is now found; he was dead but is alive." God loves his children like that good father.

Jesus told a story about a man who sent invitations to a great feast but the guests didn't come. One had bought a field, another some oxen. Another man had just got married. The host was very disappointed.

"Go and invite the beggars, the lame and the blind instead, " the man said.

Those who ignore God's teaching are just like those people who rudely ignored their invitations to the Great Feast.

Two men went to the temple to pray. One was very proud and pleased with himself and he told God this in his prayer.

The other poor man could not even lift up his eyes. He humbly prayed, "God be merciful to me a sinner." God was pleased with this prayer.

# Jesus the Saviour

One day Jesus rode into Jerusalem on a young donkey. Crowds of people joined the procession. Some cut down palm branches and put them on the ground in front of Jesus.

"Hosanna to the Son of David," the crowd shouted.
Jesus rode right into town.

Jesus and his disciples ate the Passover Feast together in a large upstairs room. Jesus broke the bread and handed it round. Then he passed round a cup of wine.

"When you eat the bread and drink the wine, remember me," said Jesus.
 Then they sang a psalm of praise.

In the garden of Gethsemane Jesus prayed to his Father. He was very troubled. The disciples slept. Judas Iscariot came and greeted Jesus with a kiss.

The soldiers had given him money to point Jesus out to them. Jesus was taken away to the High Priest's house.

Jesus was bullied and questioned. Peter waited outside. When three different people asked if he knew Jesus, he said, "No!"

At daybreak when the cockerel crowed
Jesus looked over at Peter. Peter felt
ashamed that he had denied Jesus. He
went out and cried.

Jesus was sent to Pilate the ruler, then to King Herod and back to Pilate. Herod and his servants cruelly mocked Jesus.

Pilate could find no fault with Jesus but did not let him go.

He listened to the angry crowd of people shouting, "Crucify him!"

Jesus was led away to a place called Calvary where he was nailed to a wooden cross. Jesus was not angry with those who hurt him so much.

"Father forgive them," he prayed, "for they do not understand what they are doing."

Two thieves were crucified beside Jesus. One of them knew he deserved the punishment and realised that Jesus was the Son of God. "Remember me when you come to your kingdom," he asked.

"Today you will be with me in Paradise," Jesus promised.

Jesus had forgiven his sin.

"Why have you left me alone?" Jesus called out in agony to God. He was bearing the full punishment for all the sins of his people.

Just as he died, the big curtain in the temple was torn from the top to the bottom. The rocks were split open by an earthquake.

That Friday evening two men carefully took Jesus' body down from the cross and laid him in a tomb in a garden. The tomb was a cave. A big stone had been placed across the opening of the cave.

Early on Sunday morning some ladies came
to the garden.  How surprised they were to
see the stone rolled away.

One lady ran to tell Peter and John. The others looked inside the tomb and met two angels. "Do not be afraid," one said. "Jesus is risen from the dead."

Mary Magdalene was weeping in the garden. She met a man that she thought was the gardener. "Mary," he said. Mary knew at once that he was Jesus.

Mary ran with the good news to the disciples. The disciples all saw Jesus too. He came right into the room where they were hiding and said to them, "Peace be with you."

More than five hundred people met the Lord Jesus after he had risen from the dead.

# Jesus the Real Story

ISBN: 978-1-85792-930-0
Copyright © 2004 Carine Mackenzie
Reprinted 2014
Published by Christian Focus Publications,
Geanies House, Fearn, Tain, Ross-shire, IV20 1TW,
Scotland, U.K.
www.christianfocus.com
Illustrations by Jeff Anderson
Cover design by Alister MacInnes
Printed in China